# Creepy, Crawly Caterpillars

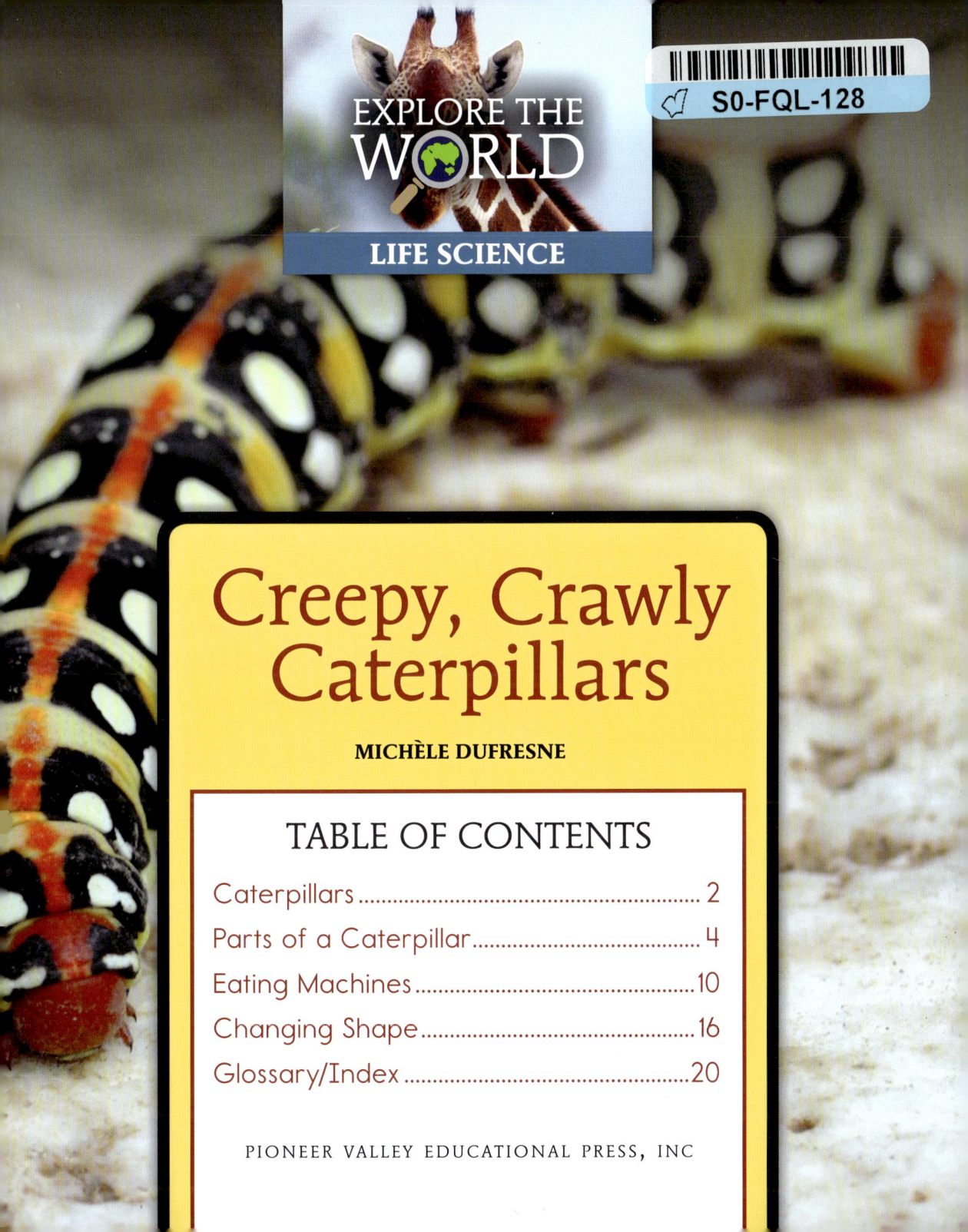

**MICHÈLE DUFRESNE**

## TABLE OF CONTENTS

Caterpillars .................................................. 2
Parts of a Caterpillar ................................... 4
Eating Machines ........................................ 10
Changing Shape ........................................ 16
Glossary/Index .......................................... 20

PIONEER VALLEY EDUCATIONAL PRESS, INC

# CATERPILLARS

Have you ever seen a caterpillar? Caterpillars look like worms but they are not. Caterpillars are baby butterflies or moths.

A butterfly or moth will lay its eggs on leaves.
A caterpillar hatches from each tiny egg.
A caterpillar will grow and change into a butterfly or a moth.

# PARTS OF A CATERPILLAR

Caterpillars come in many shapes, sizes, and colors. Some are hairy and some are smooth but their bodies all have three parts.

Caterpillars have soft bodies and they move slowly. This makes it easy for animals to catch and eat them.

Many caterpillars look like the plants or leaves that they eat. This helps protect them from **predators**.

Caterpillars are good at walking.
They can travel a long way
to look for food.
Caterpillars have six legs,
just like butterflies and moths.

You might think there are more than six legs on a caterpillar. If you pick up a caterpillar and look at its belly, you will see some stumps that look like legs. These stumps are not really legs. They are called **prolegs**. The prolegs help the caterpillar hold on as it climbs plants.

Caterpillars can have up to five pairs of prolegs.

Some caterpillars have big spots on them that look like large eyes. These are called **eyespots**. Their eyespots make them look like they have the face of a much bigger animal. The eyespots can scare away some predators.

# EATING MACHINES

A caterpillar has just one job — to eat! When caterpillars hatch from their eggs and crawl out, they begin to eat. First they will eat the eggshell. Then they begin eating a leaf. They eat a little bit at a time until almost nothing is left.

**More to Explore**
Here is a MONARCH caterpillar. It likes to eat milkweed.

Some caterpillars can be **pests**. Farmers do not like caterpillars because they eat the leaves from their plants.
They eat so much of a plant they can kill it.

**The GYPSY MOTH** caterpillar eats leaves of many kinds of trees. They eat so many leaves they can sometimes kill the trees.

**The TOMATO HORNWORM** caterpillar loves to eat tomatoes and other vegetables in the garden.

The caterpillar keeps on eating.
It grows and grows
until it is so big it can't fit
inside its skin.
When it gets too big,
it **sheds** its skin.
Most caterpillars will shed their skin
about five or six times.

15

## CHANGING SHAPE

During the next stage in a caterpillar's life, a hard shell begins to form around it. This is called a **chrysalis**.

The caterpillar hangs from a plant while the chrysalis forms.
Inside the chrysalis, the caterpillar is changing.

After about ten days, the chrysalis breaks open and out comes a butterfly or a moth!

# GLOSSARY

**chrysalis**
the hard shell that protects a moth or butterfly when it is turning into an adult

**eyespots**
something that looks like an eye

**pests**
animals that can harm something

**predator**
an animal that lives by killing and eating other animals

**prolegs**
extra legs that help a caterpillar climb

**sheds**
loses outer layer

# INDEX

abdomen 4
body parts 4
chrysalis 16–17, 18
eat 5, 10, 12–13, 14
eggs 3
eyespots 8

gypsy moth 13
head 4
monarch 10
pests 12–13
predators 5
prolegs 7

sheds 14
thorax 4
tomato hornworm 13